Y0-BRM-482

Coping™

COPING WITH

HATE AND INTOLERANCE

Avery Elizabeth Hurt

Rosen
YA™

New York

Published in 2018 by The Rosen Publishing Group, Inc.
29 East 21st Street, New York, NY 10010

First Edition

Library of Congress Cataloging-in-Publication Data

Names: Hurt, Avery Elizabeth, author.
Title: Coping with hate and intolerance / Avery Elizabeth Hurt.
Description: New York: Rosen, 2018 | Series: Coping | Includes bibliographical references and index. | Audience: Grades 7–12.
Identifiers: LCCN 2017017475 | ISBN 9781508176893 (library bound) | ISBN 9781508178507 (paperback)
Subjects: LCSH: Hate. | Toleration.
Classification: LCC BF575.H3 H87 2018 | DDC 152.4—dc23
LC record available at https://lccn.loc.gov/2017017475

Manufactured in the United States of America

CONTENTS

INTRODUCTION

In San Jose, California, a man attacked a Muslim woman and yanked off her headscarf.

A swastika and the words "Hitler" and "Jews live here" were painted on the sides of houses in Rindge, New Hampshire.

A white nationalist group distributed fliers in Milford, Connecticut.

In Omaha, Nebraska, a man stole and burned his neighbor's gay pride flag.

The words "Syrians go home and die" were painted on the wall of a school in Calgary, Alberta.

A homeless Latino man was beaten with a baseball bat by a white man yelling racial slurs in San Francisco, California.

Two gay men were brutally beaten in Austin, Texas.

A Muslim high school teacher in Georgia received an anonymous note suggesting that she hang herself with her headscarf.

Bomb threats are called into Jewish community centers across the United States.

Black churches are burned.

Elementary students chant, "Build the wall" in their lunchrooms.

The number of incidents like these is increasing in the United States according to information collected by the Southern Poverty Law Center, an organization that fights hate and intolerance and tracks both hate crimes and hate incidents. Canada is also experiencing an increase in hatred and intolerance, particularly against Muslims.

But even as intolerance and hatred grow, the response to it grows as well. People are increasingly stepping up and speaking out when they witness these incidents or are victims of them. Individuals stand up and say, "Enough is enough," and reach out to help each other. The result of this increase in hate and intolerance is a counter-increase—and a far more powerful one— of love and acceptance.

One morning in the winter of 2017, someone phoned a Jewish school in Rockville, Maryland, spewing hate and threatening to blow up the building. The school was quickly evacuated and no one was harmed, but the students, their parents, and the faculty and administration of the school were terribly frightened. Their sense of security and of belonging had been deeply shaken. No longer would they feel that just getting up and going to school was a normal,

Though acts of hate are on the rise, people all across the nation are responding by speaking out and standing up to hate.

safe thing to do. But later that day, emails, letters, and phone calls began pouring in to offer support. Religious leaders of all faiths, elected officials, and many, many citizens organized a press conference to condemn the act and demonstrate their support. Rabbi Mitchel Malkus, head of the school, wrote in an opinion piece in the *Washington Post*, "This is what Americans do in difficult times: we stand up for each other."

As you will see in the coming chapters, this is just one of many examples of how people are speaking out about hate and standing up for each other. There are many ways to safely and effectively fight hate and intolerance, whether online or in person, whether you are a bystander or a victim. And when people do confront hate with love and intolerance with acceptance, the world becomes a better place. As Rabbi Malkus wrote, "Rather than darkness and hate, a bomb threat brought light and hope for our future as a country."

CHAPTER ONE

Why Do We Hate?

I t's not hard to understand why a person might hate an individual who harmed them in some serious way or is threatening them or their loved ones—even if we can't condone that person's feelings or responses. But why do people often hate others who have done them no harm and pose no threat? Why did Dylann Roof murder nine people in a Bible study group in a Charleston, South Carolina, church? Why did a man shoot fifty-three people at a gay nightclub in Orlando, Florida? Why do school kids taunt and bully their classmates?

Choosing Sides

It's easy to condemn acts of hate and the attitudes that inspire those acts. But merely condemning hate doesn't do much to stop it. Condemnation

The Human Rights Campaign used the front of its Washington, DC, headquarters building to honor the people killed in the Orlando nightclub shooting.

without understanding can have the unfortunate result of generating even more hate. We might laugh when we catch ourselves saying something like, "I *hate* haters!" Of course, hate and intolerance must be called out and denounced whenever they show up, or they will grow and fester and many more people will be hurt. But to respond effectively, we have to develop some understanding of where hate comes from. Understanding hate is one of the first steps toward eliminating it.

The tendency to categorize people based on superficial characteristics is one of the most dangerous things in the modern world—but at one time in human history, this knack for quickly sizing people up was a lifesaving skill. Our prehistoric ancestors lived in small tribes and those tribes often competed for resources, such as food and land. People who had a tendency to be a bit cautious around outsiders may well have lived longer than people who were more open

Belonging to groups like sports teams can give us a sense of belonging, but it can be dangerous if that means discriminating against people who aren't in that group.

and accepting. But in the modern world, sizing people up and assigning them to groups and categories—particularly the categories of "us" and "them"—and making assumptions about what those people are like can lead to hate and intolerance, and in some cases even murder and war.

People have this tendency to discriminate against people who aren't part of their group, even when the groups are based on completely meaningless categories. In the 1970s, two social-psychologists, Henri Tajfel and John Turner, developed a framework called Social Identity Theory that helps us understand hate and intolerance. According to Tajfel and Turner's research, the groups people belong to—such as families, sports teams, political parties, and racial groups—are what give people a sense of belonging in the world. In order to make us feel better about ourselves, we tend to inflate the status of the group we are in and devalue the status of other groups. When you think about it, most people do this in small, mostly harmless ways quite often. For example, a fan of the New York Mets baseball team might come to believe that Mets fans are somehow better (or cooler, or nicer) people than fans of the team's archrivals, the New York Yankees; a Yankees fans may feel the same way about Mets fans. These zealous fans identify with their fellow fans and get some of their sense of who they are and how they differ from others based on that identity.

One of the important things about Tajfel and Turner's work is that it demonstrated that in modern times, identity—not just competition for resources—is important in causing people to discriminate. In the modern world, people discriminate against others not because they truly believe those others are a threat to their source of food or some other necessity of life, but because others are a threat to their sense of self-esteem or their idea of who they essentially are.

Think for a minute about the sorting hat in the Harry Potter books. The magical hat is supposed to be able to see deep inside a new Hogwarts student and determine in which house of the school that person would fit best: Gryffindor, Hufflepuff, Ravenclaw, or Slytherin. Those who live in each house have similar characteristics: Gryffindors are brave, Ravenclaws are intelligent, and so on. Of course, we learn in the books that no one is a truly perfect fit for any one house. Even the story's hero, the Gryffindor Harry Potter, turns out to have some Slytherin characteristics. And another famous Slytherin turns out to have been surprisingly brave and noble (typically a Gryffindor trait). When we step out of fiction and try to sort people in real life, we can run into problems—sometimes as serious as the problems Harry and his friends had to face.

Strong group affiliation can sometimes (though not always) lead to intolerance and even, when taken to an extreme, hate toward people who are members of

Even the Hogwarts sorting hat couldn't pin people down to one set of characteristics. Real people—and sometimes fictional ones, too—are far more complex than that.

other groups. As we saw earlier in the text, being cautious around people from different groups is probably a very natural part of being human, but it is no longer useful—and is even dangerous—in the modern world. In order for everyone to get along, we need to learn to avoid this natural tendency. People belong to plenty of different groups and have lots of different characteristics. Belonging to a certain group might mean a person has a certain skin color, speaks a certain language, wears a certain kind of clothes, eats a certain kind of food, or roots for a certain baseball team—but it says absolutely nothing about the intrinsic value of that person and is never an excuse to treat that person as less valuable than anyone else.

For some people, it can be very scary when people from other cultures move in and make changes to the way things have always been.

The Power of Fear

Identity is a powerful motivator for discrimination, but it is not as dangerous as fear. There is an old saying that if you scratch anger, you'll find fear. And the same is almost certainly true of hate. That can be hard to believe when you notice how often the victims of hate are the least powerful members of a society or culture. But the fact is, people who hate others are very often afraid of something. It may be that they are afraid of change. For example, when a lot of Asian immigrants move into a neighborhood that had mostly been filled with people of European descent, it may seem to some of the people who lived there first that their neighborhood is changing too fast and that might be a little bit scary. Most people get over this easily. They get to know their new neighbors, make new friends, learn to enjoy some new kinds of food, and share some of their favorite foods with the new people. They enjoy learning a new language and helping others learn theirs. But some people get upset because the neighborhood is different. The store on the corner that was Henry's diner for years and years is now a Korean supermarket with strange writing in the windows and unusual fruits in the bins by the door. If other things change at about the same time and some of those changes are unpleasant—for example the local factory shuts down and many people lose their jobs—people can begin to

Beyond Tolerance

Marginalized groups have been struggling against intolerance—and struggling for tolerance—for many, many years. But the word "tolerance" doesn't always strike the right note. One definition of tolerate (in the *Oxford Dictionary*) is "to allow the existence, occurrence, or practice of (something that one dislikes or disagrees with) without interference." Certainly African Americans, LGBTQ+ people, Jews, Muslims, the disabled, and the members of every other marginalized group deserve more than to be simply allowed to exist (though they certainly would appreciate being allowed to live their lives without interference).

Merriam-Webster Collegiate Dictionary defines tolerance as "sympathy or indulgence for beliefs or practices differing from or conflicting with one's own." That seems a bit closer to the mark, but still doesn't quite convey what people are asking for when they call for tolerance. What we are really trying to achieve is equality for all people, so that no matter where they came from, whom they love, what god they worship, or any other imagined or perceived difference, all people are treated equally and are given the same rights, freedoms, opportunities, and *respect* as anyone else. Words take on shades of meaning as they are used over time. When people speak of being tolerant of others, this is what they mean.

blame all that misfortune on the new people. "Things were fine before all those foreigners moved in," those people might say.

Sometimes this happens even when people aren't new, but are just different in some way from most of the other people in a society.

This is in part what happened in Germany after World War I. The German economy was in terrible shape for a lot of reasons. World War I had left Germany in ruins; the victors of that war were demanding that Germany pay huge war reparations; high tariffs, or taxes, were imposed by the United States on imports from Europe; and a worldwide economic depression devastated the economies of all nations. Some Germans, especially members of Germany's Nazi party, began to blame all this trouble on the Jews. Adolf Hitler, the dictator of Nazi Germany, proclaimed that the only way for Germany to become great again was to get rid of all the Jews. Of course this resulted in the murder of six million Jews in concentration camps. We often think of what happened in Nazi Germany as an anomaly—something that could never happen again. But in fact, genocides in which entire groups of people are persecuted and killed are all too common in the world. It has happened in Cambodia, Rwanda, Bosnia, Darfur, and many other places. It happens when hate gets out of hand. It may seem silly to compare an outbreak of schoolyard bullying or even

Thousands of Cambodians were tortured, killed, and buried in mass graves in purges during the regime of the dictator Pol Pot.

websites that post vicious things about immigrants to the mass slaughters of human beings, but if we are to prevent those extreme results of hate, we have to stop hate when it is much smaller. And one of the best places to start is very close to home.

When Is Hate a Crime?

Hate is morally repugnant, or offensive, and it is dangerous to individuals as well as to civilization. But hate in itself is not illegal and hate speech, like all speech, is protected by the United States Constitution and Canada's Charter of Rights and Freedoms. The same right to free speech that guarantees the rights of kind, loving people to say whatever they like, to wear peace symbols on their shirts, and to gather at rallies to protest intolerant policies and practices, also protects the rights of haters to wear swastikas on their shirts, to have rallies and parades in support of hate-filled agendas, and to say whatever they like, even if it is hate-filled and offensive. There are some limitations to free speech—you can't say something that entices people to commit violence, you can't say or publish obscene material, and there are some limitations

(continued on the next page)

(continued from the previous page)

on the rights students have in school—but those limitations are pretty limited.

Hate crimes are another matter entirely. The FBI defines a hate crime as a "criminal offense against a person or property motivated in whole or in part by an offender's bias against a race, religion, disability, sexual orientation, ethnicity, gender, or gender identity." When a crime is determined by the court to be a hate crime, the penalties are increased beyond what the penalty would be for a similar crime that was not motivated by hatred. Hate crimes are treated this way because hate crimes victimize not just an individual but the entire community that is made to feel vulnerable and isolated by these types of crimes.

Take a Look in the Mirror

In 2015, researchers at Utah State University studied people who had prejudices against a variety of groups (this study looked particularly at prejudices against ethnic minorities, women, homosexuals, obese people, and people struggling with substance abuse). The researchers found that people who judge and hate others have three common characteristics: they are unable to see things from the perspectives of the people they hate; they are unable to have empathy for them; and they are uncomfortable with their own emotions about being around these people. If we cannot imagine what it feels like to be someone else, the researchers found, it is much easier to hate them or be intolerant of the ways they are different from us. But perhaps the most intriguing finding of this study is that in order to overcome hate and intolerance, we have to be aware of and comfortable with our own feelings about those other people—even when those feelings aren't very nice.

In 1998, another group of scientists began a research program designed to ferret out unconscious prejudices. They designed a series of psychological tests that could determine if a person had biases or prejudices, even if that person was completely unaware of them. The research—which is still going on—has found that while very few people truly hate others, almost everyone has at least a little bit of prejudice. Some people who are very supportive of equal rights for women took the tests and discovered that they were just a tiny bit biased against women (even some women have this bias). Others who believe strongly in protecting the civil rights of LGBTQ+ Americans discovered upon taking the test that they have a slight preference for people they perceive to be straight and some discomfort with LGBTQ+ people. These findings don't suggest that most of us are secret bigots, rather that it's perfectly normal to have a few mild biases. And knowing that we have those biases can be a very good thing: if we take a good hard look at our own prejudices, we are better able to make sure those biases don't affect our behavior in negative ways. How we deal with these perfectly natural feelings of discomfort or prejudice toward people who are different from us in some way determines whether those biases lead to hate and intolerance or understanding and kindness.

For example, even though you know that only a very small percentage of Muslims are radical extremists who aim to kill other people, you still may have a twinge of anxiety when someone you suspect may be Muslim gets on a bus with you. That may not be cool, but it's not evil either. The trick is to let yourself admit that you have those feelings and then remind yourself that they aren't logical and shouldn't cause you to be unkind to perfectly innocent strangers. If you are aware of your feelings, then you might better understand why the Arab man gave you a funny look when he got on the bus. He may have been responding to the funny look you gave him—without even realizing you did it! Then you can smile and say, "hello," and what may have been an unpleasant encounter will turn into a nice one.

There is another reason it's important to be aware of our own biases, even the smallest ones. When we know that we, too, have some prejudices, we can

Being aware that we sometimes have hidden prejudices is often the best way to keep from acting on them.

better understand the prejudices of others. While it is essential to be aware of any potential biases against people who are typical victims of discrimination, it is also important to be aware of prejudices we might have toward other people, such as the people we may think are likely to hate or be intolerant of the people we do like. It's difficult to change people's attitudes by lecturing them or pointing fingers at their flaws. But often by realizing how much we all have in common, we can make progress toward eliminating hate and intolerance.

There are many reasons hate and intolerance exist in otherwise peaceful and open societies, but most of the time they all come down to a feeling of being threatened—either with literal harm (such as physical violence or loss of the means to care for oneself or one's family) or with damage to one's sense of self. When people feel threatened, they protect themselves. They put on armor, board up the windows, and close out anyone they perceive as being even a remote threat. This may be literal and obvious, such as closing the nation's borders to immigrants, refusing to serve LGBTQ+ people in restaurants, and restricting the opportunities of black people and poor people to vote; or it may be subtler, such as criticizing other people's religion or making fun of classmates who are different in some way. But in the end, these things do not make anyone any safer. They just make people lonely, isolated, and even more anxious than they were before they started boarding up their houses, their societies, and their souls.

The best way to cope with hate and intolerance, whether you are a victim or a witness, is to respond, not with more hate and aggression, but with love. If that seems like a strange idea, read on. You might be surprised to learn that the principles of nonviolent resistance to hate have a long and venerable history. Nonviolence has been used to change societies and to change the world.

CHAPTER TWO

Love Always Wins

Responding to hate with love is not a new idea. People have resisted injustice through nonviolent means for thousands of years, but in the modern sense, nonviolent resistance can be traced back to Mohandas Gandhi. He was a lawyer in India in the early twentieth century, when India was still a colony of Great Britain. Gandhi spent his life working to free India from British rule. He called for strikes, protests, and other types of peaceful civil resistance. The British sometimes responded with violence, but Gandhi urged his followers to remain peaceful, even though many other Indians who supported independence advocated rioting and other acts of violence. Gandhi was put in jail several times, but his commitment never wavered. Eventually his tactics worked and India was granted its independence in 1947.

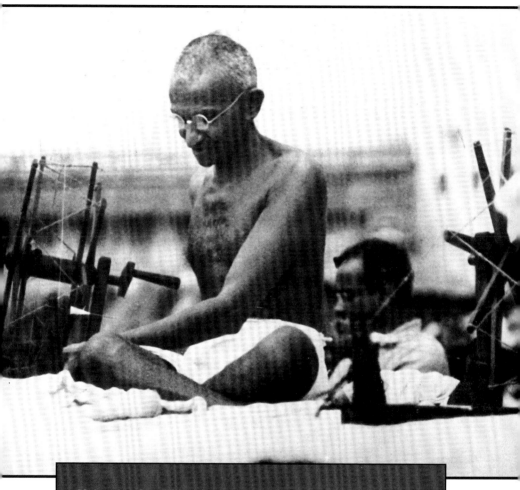

Mohandas Gandhi inspired a generation of activists to use nonviolent methods to make the world a better place.

Back in the USA

Meanwhile in the United States, African Americans were experiencing tremendous discrimination and were often the targets of hate and violence, especially

Martin Luther King Jr., leader of the American civil rights movement, leads a prayer before the march from Selma to Montgomery.

in the southern states. Martin Luther King Jr., who was the leader of the movement for justice and equality for African Americans, was deeply influenced by Gandhi. King applied Gandhi's philosophy of nonviolence and his techniques of nonviolent resistance in the long struggle for civil rights for African Americans. Sometimes it was hard for King to convince his followers that responding with love was the best and most effective way to respond to the often violent oppression they endured. King held weekly meetings to discuss the method and founded the Institute on Nonviolence and Social Change, designed to teach people that this approach was not cowardice but rather strength. In a speech about nonviolent resistance, King said, "Our aim is not to defeat the white community, not to humiliate the white community, but to win the friendship of all of the persons who had perpetrated the system in the past. The end of violence or the aftermath of violence is bitterness. The aftermath of nonviolence is reconciliation and the creation of a beloved community." King also stressed that nonviolence is as much about internal attitude as external behaviors. Not only does nonviolent resistance avoid external violence, it also avoids violence of the spirit. The heart of the method is love.

African Americans still face discrimination and even today are often the victims of hate and intolerance. But the efforts of the movement that King and others led resulted in many changes in American society; key laws, such as the Civil Rights Act of 1964 and the Voting Rights Act of 1965, protect the rights of African Americans.

Many other movements have shown the practical value of fighting hate with love. In the book *Why Civil Resistance Works: The Strategic Logic of Nonviolent Conflict*, authors Erica Chenoweth and Maria Stephan examine 323 conflicts—both violent and nonviolent—that took place around the world between 1900 and 2006. They found that nonviolent movements were twice as likely to be successful as violent ones. Nonviolence is not, however, passive. This is an important distinction. In some ways, it is even aggressive. Nonviolent resistance demands change. But it does not use violence to achieve its ends and does not respond to hate with hate. Instead it seeks to diffuse hate with love or, as King put it, "to win the friendship" of the people who hate.

Rosa Sits Down

The event that is generally considered the beginning of the civil rights movement took place one December evening in 1955 in Montgomery, Alabama. Rosa Parks, a forty-two-year-old civil rights activist, refused to give up her seat to a white man on a segregated bus. Parks was arrested and the African American community

Rosa Parks learned the techniques of nonviolent resistance from Martin Luther King Jr. and spent the rest of her life using them to change the world for the better.

responded by refusing to ride the city's buses. This was a peaceful protest (though the protestors themselves were often the victims of violence). Parks simply said, "no," when she was asked to move. When she was told she would be arrested if she didn't cooperate, she said quietly, "You can do that." Her resistance was all the more powerful—and no less intense—for being so calm. Even before the day on the bus that made Parks famous, she had worked hard for justice and equality for African Americans. She was the secretary of the Montgomery chapter of the National Association for the Advancement of Colored People (NAACP) and she organized efforts to fight injustices through the court systems. After the bus boycott and the court ruling that made bus segregation unconstitutional, Parks moved to Detroit, Michigan. There she continued to work for justice not only for American blacks, but for blacks in South Africa as well.

At first, Parks had a difficult time understanding King's approach of nonviolence. Like it did to many people in those days, responding to violence with nonviolence seemed like acceptance and even cowardice to her. But eventually she came to realize that nonviolence was more effective than violence and that love was more powerful than hate. She spent the rest of her life using nonviolent resistance to create a better world.

Malala Speaks Out

Malala Yousafzai was born in the town of Mingora in northwest Pakistan in 1997. When she was still a child, the Taliban, a militant Islamist group, took over the area. The Taliban banned television and music, and women were forbidden to go out shopping. They shut down many schools, especially schools for girls. When she was only twelve, Malala began writing a blog about what the Taliban was doing to her community, their plans to close her school, and her fears that she would be killed. She wrote under a pseudonym so that the Taliban couldn't find her and kill her, but she continued to speak out and eventually her identity became public. Nevertheless, she continued to write and speak out, arguing that all girls and women had a basic right to an education. By speaking out about the atrocities committed by the Taliban, she made sure that other factions and governments could not make deals with them or look the other way without collaborating in the evil perpetrated by the group.

Malala continued to go to school, along with other girls, and did not give in to the Taliban's pressure or the many death threats she received. One day on her way home from school, a Taliban gunman boarded the bus and shot Malala in the head. Badly injured, she was rushed to England for surgery. She survived,

When she was just a teenager, Malala Yousafzai bravely stood up to the Taliban, one of the most terrifying hate groups in the world.

and she still speaks out for women's right to an education. She was awarded the Nobel Peace Prize in 2014, when she was only seventeen years old—the youngest person ever to be given that honor. In her acceptance speech, she asked, "Why is it that countries which we call strong are so powerful in creating wars but are so weak in bringing peace? Why is it that giving guns is so easy, but giving books is so hard?"

The stories of people like Gandhi and King, Parks and Yousafzai, are inspiring and useful for mass protest movements, those calling for LGBTQ+ rights, rights for women, protection of the environment, or the end of wars. But the philosophy of nonviolent resistance is also useful when confronting hate and intolerance whenever we encounter it, even if that is just in the lunchroom.

Not in Our Town

Hate must be answered with love. Hateful actions and words must be met with actions and words that are filled with goodness. Ordinary people all over the world do this every day. In the fall of 1993, white supremacists began rampaging in the small town of Billings, Montana. They painted "Die Indian" on the homes of native Americans, vandalized Jewish cemeteries, and harassed worshippers at a black church. Then on December 5, someone threw a concrete block through the upstairs window of a Jewish home during the celebration of Hanukkah. The block destroyed a menorah belonging to five-year-old Isaac Schnitzer. This attack on young Isaac was the last straw for the town. The people of Billings responded forcefully and peacefully to this wave of hate during the holiday season. They held vigils for peace, and hundreds of people teamed up to repaint houses that had been defaced. Then people all over town—very few of whom were Jewish—bought menorahs or photocopied pictures of menorahs they found in books and displayed them in the windows of their homes and offices. When Isaac's mom drove the little boy through town to show him all the beautiful menorahs, he asked if all these people were Jewish, too. His mother told him, "No. They are friends."

A local store posted a sign that said "Not in our Town. No hate. No Violence. Peace on Earth." Since then the phrase "Not in our town" has become a rallying cry for communities all across America when hate erupts in their midst. People reach out to help each other and to stand as a community united against hate and intolerance. It is a powerful message to victims of hate that their friends and neighbors care. It is a powerful message to perpetrators of hate that their words and actions will not be accepted. And it is a powerful validation of love as a response to hate.

A Tradition of Nonviolence

Nonviolent resistance is most closely associated with Gandhi's struggle for the independence of India and with the American civil rights movement. However, there have been many other times and places when nonviolent resistance was used to protest injustice and demand change. In 1846, American philosopher and writer Henry David Thoreau expressed his opposition to slavery by refusing to pay his taxes. He was arrested and spent the night in jail. In 1872,

(continued on the next page)

(continued from the previous page)

Susan B. Anthony and fifteen other members of the women's suffrage movement cast their votes in the presidential election and were arrested for it. At a protest against the Vietnam War, held in front of the Pentagon, protesters handed flowers to the armed soldiers who had been dispatched to keep the peace. In Beijing, China, in 1989, thousands of pro-democracy protestors gathered in the city's Tiananmen Square. When the government sent tanks to disperse the protestors, one brave man walked up to the tanks, both physically and symbolically standing up to the government's tyranny.

Susan B. Anthony was persistent and courageous as she risked jail to demand that women be given the right to vote.

Take Action

If you are a victim of hate and intolerance or a witness to it— whether those acts are large ones, like what happened in Billings, or small ones, such as rudeness or insulting comments—there are very concrete actions you can take. The first step is to do something. Hate and intolerance thrive when they are ignored or accepted. Telling perpetrators of hate, "not in our neighborhood, not in our school, not on our team," can stop hate in its tracks.

Acts of hate and intolerance must always be reported. If it happens at school, tell a teacher. If it happens in the community, tell a trusted adult. But it's also important for individuals to speak up on the spot when they witness or are the victims. This doesn't have to be confrontational. When someone tells a racist or sexist joke, you can simply say, "I didn't think that was funny. It

Sometimes people don't even realize that what they've said is hateful or offensive. You can often stop hate in its tracks by simply and kindly pointing out words that hurt.

is hurtful to many people;" if you are a member of the targeted group, you can say, "That was hurtful; please don't make jokes about me and my people."

It is important to stand up to such comments even when no one of the targeted group is around. Ignoring hurtful comments and behavior signals that you are okay with it as long as no one who might be offended is around. Hate and intolerance thrives and grows in the shadows until people are brave enough to say these things out loud.

You can also speak up by modeling kindness and love. Showing respect for others can quickly spread and become the norm in a school or neighborhood. Many people who practice intolerance do so not because they have strong feelings against particular groups, but because that's simply the way they've seen others behave. Sadly, intolerance can often become a habit when people repeat what they hear others say and adopt those attitudes without carefully thinking them through. By nudging the culture of your school or community away from hate and intolerance and toward love and inclusiveness, you can make a dramatic difference. Using non-offensive language and making friends with all the people in your school and community will set examples for others without having to preach or lecture. When confronting intolerance and hateful language, it can be very helpful to approach the problem with kindness. Instead of saying "You are a mean person" or "racists are ignorant!" you might instead say, "I think it's cool to treat everyone with respect" or "I deserve to be treated with respect."

When a hate incident happens—say some kids painted racist slurs on a wall of the school—rather than confronting the people who defaced the wall, instead get together a group of classmates and neighbors (as many as you can find) and wash and repaint the wall. If people are making fun of a disabled classmate as he sits alone at lunch, get together several other kids and join him at his table. If a bully pushes a lesbian student and makes her drop her books, stop and help her pick them up; then, walk with her to her next class or ask her to join you and your friends at your table during lunch. If you're the victim of these kinds of acts, reach out for help and support. Though it may not always seem that way, there are more good people in the world than bad. And the more good examples people have to follow, the sooner they will join the movement to defeat hate with love and kindness.

There are also a few organized practices schools often use that can help create a culture of kindness rather than intolerance. Mix It Up at Lunch Day is an event sponsored by Teaching Tolerance (a program of the Southern Poverty Law Center) and held on the last Tuesday of October each year. It's simple: students who

Teenage girls get together to clean up graffiti in their Los Angeles neighborhood.

participate connect with someone new at lunch by moving from the place where they normally sit to another spot. It's a very gentle way to break down social barriers and to make new friends.

You might also consider taking part in the Great Kindness Challenge, a week in which people try to commit as many acts of kindness as possible. You can focus especially on acts that defuse hate and intolerance, such as saying hello to people in their native language, inviting someone who has been shunned by others at school or in the neighborhood to join you for lunch or come over for dinner, welcoming immigrants and new students to your school, or asking people who are often the victims of intolerance to tell you more about their cultures. The national Great Kindness Challenge is typically observed in the last week of January (you can find out more at thegreatkindnesschallenge.com), but schools can do it whenever it is convenient, and individuals can to it every day. Of course, it is crucial to not put yourself or anyone else in harm's way. But there are safe and effective actions you can take. In Chapter Four we will see lots of exciting and effective ways people are responding to and coping with hate and intolerance, but first let's take a look at hate's latest playground: the World Wide Web.

Myths & **FACTS**
About Hate and Intolerance

Myth: Bigotry is just a part of being human. There is nothing we can do to change that.

Fact: Though it is true that humans have a natural tendency to classify people into groups and to see those groups as "us" and "them," it is by no means impossible to get over this tendency. Humans are influenced by their minds and their cultures as well as by their genes. That's why it is so important to examine these prejudices so that we take charge of our behaviors rather than letting our behaviors be in charge of us.

Myth: The election of Barack Obama, the nation's first black president, means that racism in America is over.

Fact: While the election of the first African American president of the United States was a major step for the United States, it did not signal an end to racism. As wonderful as it is that more African Americans, LGBTQ+ citizens, and other minorities are serving their country in

(continued on the next page)

Myths & FACTS

(continued from the previous page)

elected offices both locally and nationally, members of these communities are still not being treated equally throughout the nation, and patterns of intolerance and incidents of hate continue.

Myth: Challenging bigotry is just another form of bigotry.

Fact: People who are members of majority groups in society often claim that when minority groups demand equal rights, they are demanding special privileges and thus infringing on the rights of the majority group. However, the demand to be given the same rights, respect, and dignity as anyone else is not a demand for special treatment; it is a demand for equal treatment. No one's rights are being infringed upon when every person is given equal rights and respect.

Virtual Hate

The internet—and particularly the World Wide Web—has provided previously unimagined opportunities for sharing and accessing information, for exploring the world, and for connecting with other people. There is hardly a subject you can't learn more about through astute use of the web and hardly a place you can't (virtually) visit. The web has the power to bring the world together. Thanks to the web, it's easier to stay in touch with the people you love. You can make new friends all over the world and easily learn about their homes and cultures. The web has made it much easier to learn and practice foreign languages. The web has, in many ways, broken down national and cultural barriers.

But the same virtual world that keeps us in touch and informed, and gives us funny cat videos, is also a fertile breeding ground for hate and intolerance. It is a world where anyone can say anything—no matter how hurtful or dangerous—

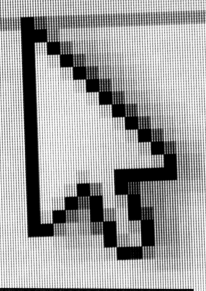

Like any tool, the internet can be used to do good or bad things. By using the internet wisely, you can help make it a force for good.

and have that message spread around the world at very nearly the speed of light. It is a world where lies come packaged in the same form as truth, and it is increasingly difficult to tell them apart.

Like any technology, the web can be used for good or ill. Without the web, the outside world would not have known about Malala Yousafzai and her struggle to protect the rights of girls to an education. Without the web, many of the acts of hate and intolerance would only be known to the few people who are directly affected, making it harder for the rest of the world to help. Knowing how to use the web wisely and well and how to be a good and responsible citizen of the virtual world can tip the power of the internet from those who would use it to spread hate to those who use it to spread love and inclusion.

They Can't Say That, Can They?

The obvious solution to online hate is to ban it. But as we have seen, that is not necessarily a good idea. Free speech is an essential feature of democracy and is vigorously protected in many nations, including the United States and Canada. Imposing limits on the freedom of citizens to express themselves can quickly go from protecting citizens from hate to giving the haters a powerful tool to restrict the voices of those who disagree with them. At times when even people at the highest levels of government are engaging in and spreading hate speech, it becomes even more important to protect the rights of anyone to speak up freely and without fear of reprisal. Limiting the rights of those we disagree with all too often ends up limiting our own rights. The largest and most powerful US organization dedicated to the protection of individual rights and liberties, the American Civil Liberties Union (ACLU), has gone to court to protect the right of Nazis to parade. This is not because the ACLU agrees with what Nazis have to say or is unconcerned about the spread of their hateful message, but because the organization understands that restricting anyone's right to freedom of expression is a threat to everyone's right. There are better ways to fight hate speech than by banning it.

In any case, policing speech on the web is extremely difficult. However, popular social networking sites, such as Facebook, Twitter, and Instagram, have some systems

Eva-Maria Kirschsieper, head of public policy at Facebook, Inc., attends a conference on combating political hate speech and fake news on social media in Berlin, Germany, in 2017.

in place to restrict the worst excesses of online hate speech. Defining hate speech poses difficulties as well—the line between expressing hate and expressing an opinion is not always easy to draw. But even though we can't prevent people from posting hateful messages online, there is a great deal we can do to limit its influence.

Not in My Feed

It's a common enough experience. You get up one morning, open your Facebook or Instagram account, and find a racist joke, a swastika, or a post that demeans immigrants or threatens Muslims. What do you do? Do you respond with a well-reasoned argument for why you find this offensive? Do you unfriend or block the person who made the post? What if the person is someone you know well, such as a friend or family member? What if the hateful post is directed particularly at you or a group you belong to? What then?

If the post is truly hateful, you can and should flag it. Most social media sites have a means for flagging offensive posts and a procedure for reviewing these. If they are deemed truly offensive, the post is deleted, and, in extreme cases, the poster's account may be suspended or canceled. If you are personally

It can be shocking and disturbing to open your social media feed and find hate speech, but it happens all the time.

threatened by someone online or feel that you are in danger of being harmed, immediately report this to the site where the threat was posted, inform a trusted adult, and if the threat is specific, call the police. If you see something online that promotes violence or serious destruction of property, you can report it to Fight Against Hate, at fightagainsthate.com.

Blocking or unfriending those you merely disagree with is not always the best approach. These days many people live in what experts call "information bubbles." They see only the opinions they already agree with. This can be very soothing and comforting, but it also puts up more walls between people and keeps us from learning about each other. If people are simply spewing hate, then by all means report and block them. But when people are expressing opinions that are merely different from yours, it might be valuable to hear them out—even if those opinions offend you in some cases. It's never a good idea to listen to or pass on nasty posts, but if someone voted for a different candidate, is a member of a different political party, or identifies with a different religious group, then keeping the channels of communication open is always a good idea. As we saw in Chapter One, making friends with the people we are trying to persuade is key to success. How can you expect others to listen to your opinions if you don't listen to theirs?

More Speech

Another way to fight hate online is by countering it with better messages. You don't have to respond directly to, say, a racist joke or a post demeaning immigrants or LGBTQ+ people. Just find some positive information about the issue and post that on your feed. A link to a story about immigrants who are improving their new community or a gay couple who have adopted a baby can counter the negative perceptions other people may be spreading about these groups. The ACLU placed an ad in Times Square that showed a Muslim woman in a hijab standing in front of a building painted with graffiti saying, "Muslims, go home." The image was followed by images of people holding signs that said, "Support Freedom of Religion," "Love thy Neighbor," and the message, "Fight Hate Speech with More Speech." Individuals can use their social media accounts to fight hate speech with more speech by posting positive encouraging messages (such as the signs in the ad), positive images of people who are often the victims of hate, or uplifting, inclusive messages. Good messages can go viral just as easily as hateful messages, and the impact can be just as strong. In their book *Viral Hate: Containing Its Spread on the Internet*, Abraham Foxman and Christopher Wolf tell the story of a post that appeared on Facebook in 2010 announcing a new

It's easy to be taken in by fake news—it has happened to almost everyone—but you can learn to be savvy about what you read.

event to take place over two weeks that July. It was "Kill a Jew Day," which encouraged followers to commit acts of violence toward Jews wherever they saw them. Followers of the site responded with many hate-filled, anti-Semitic rants and screeds (long speeches or writings). Facebook responded to complaints and disabled the page. (Speech that incites violence is not protected by the US Constitution or Canada's Charter of Rights and Freedoms.) But before that process was complete, the Facebook community mounted a response of its own, fighting hate speech with more speech. Another event page was quickly posted. This one was "One Million Strong Against Kill a Jew Day." Responses like this are actually quite powerful. They show in no uncertain terms that there is more love than hate in the world and that for every hateful post there are millions of people who will stand up and speak out against it.

True or False

Fake news has been around a long time. During the American Revolution, in an attempt to get more people to join the cause, patriots spread false news claiming that King George was sending thousands of soldiers to murder colonists. In the 1800 US presidential election between Thomas Jefferson and John Adams, the press was filled with outlandish fake news stories about both candidates. Even so, thanks to the internet, it is much easier now for fake news to reach a lot of people before anyone has had time to check it out and point out that it isn't true. Social media sites are trying to crack down on fake news sites, but the best way to protect yourself from fake news is to learn how to tell truth from fiction. That's not always as easy as it sounds. A 2017 survey

A little practice and some good sleuthing will help you learn to spot fake news when you see it—before you re-post or share.

by Common Sense Media found that less than 45 percent of Americans ages ten to eighteen thought that they were able to identify fake news in their social media feeds. A few techniques can help you sort fact from fiction on the web.

Your teachers probably tell you to cite your sources when you make claims in a research paper. Demand the same of the stories you believe or share online. First find out where the news came from. Was it a legitimate news source, such as the *Washington Post*, the *New York Times*, or your hometown paper? Newspapers like these do occasionally make mistakes, but when they do, they correct them as soon as the mistake is discovered. They also print and post opinion pieces—articles that go beyond just reporting the facts and include the author's opinion and the facts. But even these authors are required to back up their opinions with verifiable facts. Sometimes it is not so obvious if a news outlet is legitimate or not. "Trump Orders All White House Phones Covered in Tin Foil" was a headline that ran in the "Borowitz Report," an online column that is hosted by the *New Yorker*, a very reputable magazine. But if you look closely, you'll see that at the top of the page where the article appears, it says "Satire from the Borowitz Report." Satire,

Andy Borowitz is the author of the satirical column "The Borowitz Report," hosted on the website of the *New Yorker*.

of course, uses humor and exaggeration to entertain or make political statements. Satire is nothing new, either. In his 1729 essay "A Modest Proposal," Jonathan Swift suggested a foolproof method of "preventing the children of poor people from being a burden to their parents or country": sell them for food to rich English people. This over-the-top satire was designed to condemn the practices of the English toward the Irish, but some people still thought Swift was serious.

Always be sure to read the entire article before you share it on social media. An exciting (or outrageous) headline might grab your attention, but the article that follows might not be what you expected—or would want to share. Often attention-getting headlines are designed just to get you to repost them and the content is more nonsense than not. If you're still suspicious that an article may be bogus, use Google or another search engine to find out more about the author. Is it a legitimate journalist or expert? Or does this name appear at the top of yet more sketchy-looking articles and on more questionable sites? When you read the article, look for misspelled words and poor grammar. Use your critical thinking skills to determine if the writer's argument makes sense. When possible, double-check the facts. A widely circulated graphic headlined "US Crime Statistics 2015" cited homicide statistics based on race. Almost all of the data in this graphic was false. The real information is available to the public on the FBI website and can be easily checked out.

As we saw in Chapter Two, it can be difficult to recognize our own biases. We all have them, however, to one degree or another, and we all tend to believe posts and news items that support our biases ("I knew it all along") and not believe those that don't ("oh, that's rubbish!"). Being highly aware of your pre-existing beliefs can keep you from being suckered by false news stories that support those beliefs.

One way to inoculate yourself against fake news is to be very well informed. Find a source of news that you trust (preferably one that does not have a strong bias in any direction) and read it regularly. Being familiar with real news (and the conventions of real reporting) will make it easier to spot the fake kind. Legitimate news sources will typically list their physical location, the names of their editors, and contact information somewhere on their websites. If this is missing, that should raise a red flag about the site. The more you practice evaluating news, the better you'll get at spotting the fakes. But when you're not sure, there are several reputable sites that fact-check news stories and information making the rounds on the web. Snopes.com, politifact.com, and factcheck.org may have already confirmed or debunked an item you're wondering about. Abraham Lincoln really didn't say, "Half of what you read on the

If Abraham Lincoln were alive today, he really might say that "half of what you read on the internet is a lie."

internet is a lie," but if he had lived long enough to see the internet, he might have.

Though the internet can be a hotbed of hate and a swamp of fake news and outrageous lies, it can also be a powerful force for good. In March 2017, vandals broke into the Islamic Center of Tucson, Arizona, and destroyed many copies of the Quran, the Muslim holy book. Nothing was stolen; it was clearly an act of vandalism and hate. The community responded with an outpouring of support. And then they turned to the web. A local Jewish citizen began an online campaign to raise money to replace the damaged holy books. The request for funds read in part: "There are Jews, Christians, Buddhists, Hindus, Sikhs, Baháʾí, Atheists, Agnostics and others in Tucson who love our Muslim brothers and sisters. Though we may have different beliefs, we want them to be safe and never to have to pray in fear. Let's come

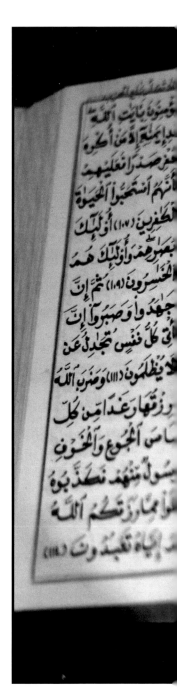

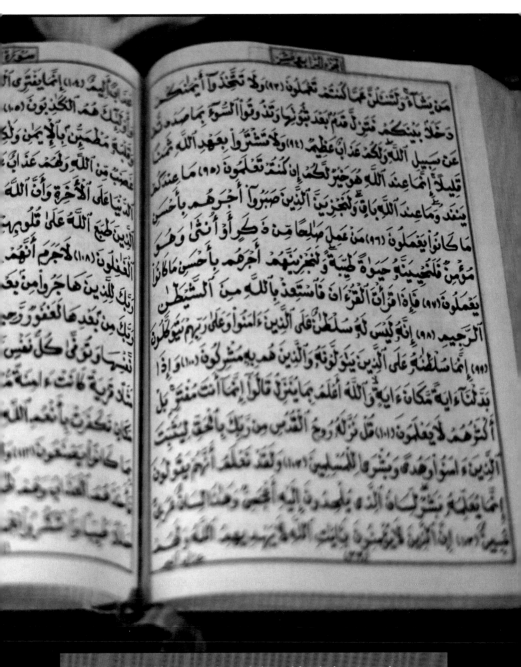

Good online citizens used a web-based fundraiser to replace copies of the Quran that were damaged in an act of hate and vandalism.

together and replace the damaged copies of the Holy Quran and show our Muslim neighbors that they are indeed our brothers and sisters." The campaign raised enough money to not only replace the copies of the Quran, but to upgrade the Islamic Center's security system as well. Good online citizens are much like good citizens anywhere else: they are responsible about what they say and how they interact with others; they speak up about injustice or intolerance when they see it; and they reach out to help each other when they are in need.

10 Great Questions to Ask a Social Media Expert

1. Many of my friends on Facebook post bigoted material, but they pretend they're just jokes and say I'm being oversensitive when it bothers me. How can I respond?

2. Both of my parents are naturalized citizens who were born in Iran. So far, everything has been fine, but I keep seeing posts online that make me fear for their safety. Do I have to wait until we are actually threatened to do something?

3. I have flagged inappropriate content on several social media sites, but it doesn't seem to do any good. More offensive material just keeps popping up. Will we ever be able to put a stop to this?

4. When I see hateful posts online, I immediately unfriend the person who posted it. Isn't it better to just ignore this kind of thing? Won't responding just encourage it?

5. I attend a very diverse school and everyone I know is kind and decent. I've been reading a lot about an increase in hate speech and hate crimes, but I haven't seen any of it personally. Is this being overblown?

(continued on the next page)

10 Great Questions to Ask a Social Media Expert

(continued from the previous page)

6. Everyone is warning me about fake news—but how do I know that the news on the professional sites is true? Couldn't the major news outlets be spreading fake news, too?

7. The person who shares the most hateful material on my social media feed is my grandfather. How can I let him know that I don't like this stuff without being disrespectful?

8. My school installed filters on the computers we use to access the internet. I think it is a good idea to try to protect us from hate speech online, but don't the filters violate our rights?

9. I want to do more about hate online than just flag, block, and unfriend. What can I do that makes a positive difference?

10. After five minutes online, I get totally discouraged about the state of the world. What can you tell me to give me hope?

CHAPTER FOUR

A Brighter Future

I t would be both perilous and naive to downplay the serious injustices and acts of hate and intolerance that so many people face these days. But the news is not all bad. Despite a short-term increase in acts of hate and intolerance, the outlook for the long term is promising.

There have always been periods in history that have experienced outbreaks of bigotry. For example, in the years just after World War I, the United States withdrew into dangerous isolationism, nativism, and religious fundamentalism. Hate groups flourished. The Ku Klux Klan, which was formed at the end of the Civil War, had died out by the 1870s but was resurrected in 1915. The group made a powerful comeback, becoming very active in the 1920s not only in the rural South, but also in many cities around the nation. This time it targeted

The Ku Klux Klan made a comeback in the 1920s, during a time of isolationism and xenophobia. The organization is still somewhat active today.

Catholics, Jews, and immigrants as well as African Americans. What today we would call hate crimes increased dramatically in those years. While hate and discrimination never ended, the 1930s and 1940s saw a great deal of progress for previously marginalized groups, laying the groundwork for the civil rights advances of the 1950s and 1960s.

Now we find ourselves in yet another period of increased hate and intolerance. This time, however, things are different. Though some people are spreading hate, even more people are standing up and challenging that hate. Western society is becoming far less accepting of intolerance and bigotry. There was a time in our society when acts of hatred and violence would very often go unremarked. Reporting such incidents was almost unheard of and the authorities had very little reason for acting even when they were informed.

Not too long ago, bullying was considered a normal part of growing up—a rite of passage and something kids just had to deal with. Today schools organize anti-bullying task forces, leaders enact anti-bullying policies, and teachers and administrators are trained in recognizing and responding to acts of bullying. Victims of bullying are supported and protected; they are not expected to just accept it as a part of life.

Not that many years ago, kids could paint swastikas on the side of a house or school and the authorities wouldn't go to much trouble to find out who was responsible; if anyone knew who was responsible, they were not likely to turn in the offenders. In the past, people who did want to intervene when they witnessed acts of bigotry often did not know what to do, or they weren't sure what actions would be both effective and safe. Now, as we shall see, there are organizations dedicated to training ordinary people in the best ways to stand up to bigotry. Even though hate and intolerance is on the rise, love and acceptance are on the rise, too. And love and acceptance has a great deal more momentum than we often realize.

A More Peaceful World

In his 2011 book, *The Better Angels of Our Nature*, cognitive scientist and author Steven Pinker makes a strong case that we are living in the most peaceful time in the history of civilization. He argues that this is not an anomaly, but a trend. Pinker called the period after World War II "the long peace" and the time after the fall of communism the "new peace." Neither of these periods were or are free from war—or other kinds of violence—but as Pinker demonstrates with reams of data, they were far more peaceful than any previous period in history. Why? At least in part it is because people all over the world, but especially in the West, were championing human rights and speaking out against everyday aggressions, such as the ones we've been discussing in this book, like they never had before. Pinker does not claim that humans have become angels or that violence has disappeared, but he provides a great deal of evidence that people are much kinder and more tolerant than they've ever been. And what's even more important, he argues that we are continuing to become so. Despite small and local setbacks, the world really is becoming a more peaceful place.

So how does a society prevent or reverse these outbreaks of intolerance when they occur? One way is by learning from the past. In an opinion piece that circulated widely on the web, Sabine Heinlein, a German American, tells Americans that when she was growing up in Germany, she was taught that "the reason why Adolf Hitler was able to rise to power was that no one stood up for the Jews." As a result, modern Germans are very conscious of the responsibility to keep intolerance and hate from breeding in society.

Like the United States, Germany, too, is experiencing a resurgence of intolerance; Heinlein urges people of all nations to speak up and reach out when they witness or experience hate and intolerance.

And people are doing just that—in new and creative ways.

The Three Ds

Sometimes people are complacent in the face of bigotry not because they don't care, but because they have no idea what to do. They may be afraid of getting hurt, of making the situation worse, or perhaps of escalating a minor incident into a major one and turning a hateful comment into a violent act. This is a valid concern. Fortunately, there are now groups who train people to respond to such incidents in the best way possible. A method that has been very useful for people who are witnesses, but are not the targets of acts of hate and violence, is called the Three Ds of Bystander Intervention.

The first D, distraction, is simply to try to stop the incident by creating a distraction. Say someone is calling a person insulting names in the hall at school. You could walk up to either the person who's being harassed or the harasser,

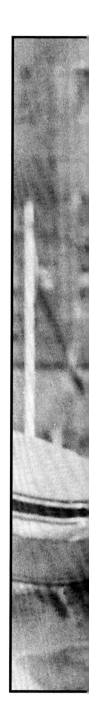

Hitler might not have come to power if more people had spoken up and challenged his racist rants. That's a lesson for us today.

and just interrupt. "Excuse me, but did you get our homework assignment for math class?" Or stick out your hand and say, "Aren't you in my English class? I don't believe we've met." It doesn't have to be anything that really makes sense (maybe you know for sure that person isn't in your English class!); it's just a way to interrupt what's going on. Another option—and this is especially useful when you really don't know any of the people involved—is to do something that grabs everyone's attention. Drop your books or shopping bag, stumble and bump into a chair, or break into a sneezing fit. These things may sound kind of silly, but may be all it takes to diffuse a potentially bad situation before any damage is done—without adding any risk to yourself or additional risk to the victim.

The second D, delegate, means getting someone else to help out. Go find a teacher or an older student or a parent; let someone with more authority or social status know what's happening. Oftentimes hateful acts breed quietly behind the scenes. People who are in charge wouldn't allow it to continue if they knew it was happening, but as long as they don't know, the incidents not only happen but also become more numerous. Delegating is especially important if it looks like the situation might become violent.

Delay is the third D. This actually refers to situations where you weren't around when the initial incident happened (or for whatever reason weren't

Strange as it sounds, dropping a pile of books might be just the thing to create a diversion and dissolve a hateful incident.

able to stop it). In this case, you do something after. For example, someone pushes another person off the sidewalk and says, "outta my way, queer." In this case, you walk up to the person who's just been abused and ask if he's okay, see if he needs any help. Other things that come under "delay" are when you help neighbors clean up after their property has been defaced or tape a welcome note to the locker of a new student or the door of new neighbors who have experienced abuse because of their race, religion, or sexual orientation. It's delay when you tell a classmate who's been bullied for being fat that she looks nice today. In this case, delay doesn't mean putting something off; it means following up and continuing to help even after the incident it over.

None of these tactics seems very heroic, but they are. Heroes don't always wear capes, and they almost never use violence to save the day. Heroes notice when people are in trouble and they do something to help, even when that something isn't flashy.

Legislative Landmarks

The future looks bright for those who are working for a more tolerant and inclusive world. But when things feel discouraging, it can be inspiring to look back at just a few of the legislative gains that have been made over the years.

1964—The Civil Rights Act was passed. This legislation ended racial segregation in public places and banned employment discrimination based on race, color, sex, religion, or national origin.

1965—The Voting Rights Act of 1965 not only outlawed poll taxes and literacy requirements that had been used by Southern states to prevent blacks from voting, but it also required states with a history of voter suppression to get federal approval before making changes to their voting laws and procedures. (Distressingly, this last provision was struck down by the Supreme Court in 2013, but its other provisions remain in place.)

2009—The Hate Crimes Prevention Act was signed into law in the United States. This federal law gives the US Department of Justice the authority to prosecute crimes that were motivated by the victims' actual or perceived race, color, religion, national origin, gender, sexual orientation, gender identity, or disability.

2015—The Supreme Court of the United States ruled that laws preventing same sex couples from marrying are unconstitutional.

Speaking Up Loud and Softly

When you try to resist bigotry, it can seem like you are all alone. But in truth, people all over the world are standing up to the recent surge in hate and intolerance and making it very clear that this is no longer accepted in our society. These efforts range from small local acts of kindness and respect to huge political movements.

In 2007, in a small school in rural Nova Scotia, Canada, a ninth-grade boy wore a pink polo shirt to his first day of school. Some other boys bullied him, calling him a homosexual for wearing pink. They threatened to beat him up. Two older boys—in grade twelve—heard about this harassment and decided, as one of them put it, "enough is enough." The boys bought fifty pink shirts and tank tops, then recruited friends and classmates to get on board with the plan. The next day far more than fifty students arrived wearing pink (many, hearing of the plan, wore their own pink clothing). The message of support was clear to the student who had been bullied and it was equally clear to the bullies that they had no support. And no one had to beat up anyone.

In Philadelphia, after a Jewish cemetery was vandalized, the Philadelphia Building and Construction Council announced that it would replace the damaged headstones at no charge. A local

Sometimes standing up to hate is as simple as just wearing a pink shirt to school.

electrical workers union volunteered to install security lighting at the cemetery. A group of Christian, Muslim, and Jewish religious leaders held a press conference to denounce the acts of violence and reinforce their support for each other.

Noting that many immigrants facing deportation actually win their cases when they have legal representation, many groups have organized to raise money to pay the legal fees of these immigrants. Many lawyers have offered their services for free.

Standing up to hate groups can be dangerous, but there are safe ways to do it. The Southern Poverty Law Center, an organization dedicated to fighting hate and bigotry, strongly advises against attending hate rallies and marches in order to protest them. Not only is that not safe, it just increases attendance at the rally. A safer and more effective response is to stage a counter rally. If there is an anti-immigrant rally in your town, organize a welcome rally at a nearby venue. If the Ku Klux Klan is marching in your town, make no attempt to interfere (it is their legal right to march), but simply organize an anti-hate march on another street. Fighting hate speech with more speech is not just an online strategy, it can be powerful in the real world as well.

As important as it is to not give too much publicity to people who spread hate, it is equally

No More Us and Them

There are many minority groups in the United States, but when you add them all together, the number of people who are not members of the majority is pretty large. According the US Census, the number of people who belong to a non-white minority group will be greater than the number of whites by the middle of the century. The United States—as well as many other Western nations—is rapidly becoming a majority minority nation.

Like any cultural change, this transition can be difficult. Greater numbers does not mean more political power. When the dominant group begins to lose its majority, there is often a great deal of push-back and often a sharp, if temporary, rise in intolerance for other groups. The trend, however, is encouraging. The more minority citizens there are, then the more votes they have, the more chances they have to take part in government, and the more they are chosen to serve their nation in elected office. As new generations grow up in a world filled with a great variety of people—different colors, races, nationalities, genders, sexual orientations—a diverse world will become the norm and reasons to hate each other will diminish. No more "us" and "them." Just many different types of "us."

important that good people know what is going on. In fact, one of the reasons so many people are standing up and speaking out against hate and intolerance is that they are more aware now when it happens. That's why it is a good idea to let the press as well as the authorities know. For example, say someone paints swastikas and offensive language on the locker room at a neighborhood baseball field. You can gather a group of people—as many as you can find—to come out and wash the offending words and images off the wall. But call the city government and the local newspaper, too, and let them know what's going on. The press will report not only that this hate incident happened, but also what people did about it. It will serve both as a call to action against hate and an inspiring story of how to respond.

Love Will Win

If we want a future that is free of hate and intolerance, we can have one. But we have to make that happen. It requires that we speak up and reach out. Martin

Be sure to let the press know when you respond to hate with love. The publicity will inspire others to join in.

Niemöller was a clergyman in Nazi Germany who became an outspoken critic of Adolf Hitler, though he had once been a committed nationalist. After the war,

Pastor Martin Niemöller was an outspoken critic of Hitler and the Nazi Party, and he has inspired many others to speak up when they see hate and injustice.

Niemöller made many speeches about the fact that it took so long for the German people, himself included, to speak out about what was happening to the Jews during Hitler's rule. He spent the last seven years of Hitler's rule in a concentration camp. Later, he said,

>First they came for the Socialists, and I did not speak out—
>Because I was not a Socialist.
>Then they came for the Trade Unionists, and I did not speak out—
>Because I was not a Trade Unionist.
>Then they came for the Jews, and I did not speak out—
>Because I was not a Jew.
>Then they came for me—and there was no one left to speak for me.

Niemöller's words are a powerful reminder to us all how important it is to speak up for others, and not to wait or think that if we ignore hate, it will go away. It will go away, but only if we refuse to allow it in our midst.

A quick glance at the headlines shows that acts of hate and intolerance are increasing. But you don't have to dig too deep into the news to see that acts of love and acceptance are increasing as well. As we saw in Chapter Two, people are able to feel hate only when they can't feel what others feel, can't imagine what it

We can live in a world without hate—we just have to reach out to each other.

feels like to be someone else. By reaching out to others when they are in need—cleaning their walls; rebuilding their churches; picking up their school books; visiting their churches, synagogues, and mosques and inviting them to our sacred places; learning their languages and teaching them ours—we can share each others' grief and each others' joy. Hate cannot long live in a land where people hold each others' hands.

Glossary

affiliation The state of being officially a part of or connected with a group or organization.

anomaly Something that is different from what it normal, routine, or expected.

anti-Semitic Prejudice or hostile actions directed toward Jews.

atrocity An exceptionally bad or cruel act, usually involving physical violence.

bias Prejudice; a position (well-supported or not) in favor of or against something.

bigot Someone who treats members of certain groups with hatred or intolerance.

complacent Being satisfied with how things are, unwilling to stir oneself to try to achieve change.

confrontational Relating to an action or response that seems intended to created conflict or violence.

dictator A ruler who has complete control of a government and/or society, often an oppressive ruler.

empathy The ability to imagine the feelings of others.

ethnic Relating to a group of people, within a larger population, that are categorized by cultural characteristics, such as race, religion, language, or nation of origin.

faction A group, such as in politics, that disagrees with another group.

fundamentalism An excessively strict adherence to the basic tenets or scriptures of a religion or ideology.

genocide The murder of a large group of people, particularly those of an ethnic group or nationality.

Hanukkah A minor Jewish Holiday beginning on the 25th of the month of Kislev in the Jewish calendar, and lasting eight days.

hijab A head covering worn by some Muslim women.

intrinsic Being a natural or essential part of something.

isolationism The policy or practice of a nation to refrain from involvement in the affairs of other nations.

menorah A sacred nine-branched candelabra, used for celebrating Hanukkah. (Also refers to a seven-branched candelabra used in other ceremonies.)

nativism The policy or practice of providing the rights and interests of native born citizens over those of immigrants.

pseudonym A made-up name used to conceal or protect the identity of the user, often a writer.

reparations Financial or other compensation made to the victors in war by the defeated nation or nations.

reprisal Retaliation, as for an insult, damages, or other harm, perceived or real.

reputable Generally held in high esteem; having a good reputation.

segregated Isolated, divided, or kept apart, as when races are kept separate in society.

swastika An ancient symbol adopted for use by the German Nazi party and later used by anti-Semites and white supremacists in the United States.

venerable Greatly respected, usually because of age, experience, and achievement.

For More Information

American Civil Liberties Union

125 Broad Street, 18th Floor

New York, NY 10001

(212) 549-2500

Website: aclu.org

Facebook: @ aclu.nationwide

Twitter: @ACLU

The ACLU is an organization that works to defend and protect the individual rights and liberties that are guaranteed by the Constitution of the United States.

Anti-Defamation League

1100 Connecticut Avenue, NW, #1020

Washington, DC 20036

(202) 452-8310

Website: adl.org

Facebook: @anti.defamation.league

Twitter: @ADL_National

Instagram: @adl_national

The ADL is an international organization that fights anti-Semitism and all other hate. See website for information on the office nearest you.

Canadian Civil Liberties Association

90 Eglinton Avenue E

Toronto, ON M4P 2Y3

Canada

(416) 363-0321

Email: mail@ccla.org

Website: ccla.org

Facebook: @cancivlib

Twitter: @cancivlib

The Canadian Civil Liberties Association is an organization fighting for the civil liberties, human rights, and democratic freedoms of people all across Canada.

Leadership Conference on Civil and Human Rights

1620 L Street NW Suite 11000

Washington, DC 20036

(202) 466-3434

Website: civilrights.org

Facebook: @ civilandhumanrights

Twitter: @civilrightsorg

The Leadership Conference on Civil and Human Rights is a coalition of more than two hundred organizations working to promote and protect the civil and human rights of all people in the United States.

Media Smarts: Canada's Centre for Digital and Media Literacy
205 Catherine Street, Suite 100
Ottawa, ON K2P 1C3
Canada
(613) 224-7721
Email: info@mediasmarts.ca
Website: mediasmarts.ca
Facebook: @MediaSmarts
Twitter: @MediaSmarts
Media Smarts is an organization dedicated to ensuring that children and youth have the critical thinking skills necessary to engage with media as active and informed digital citizens.

Southern Christian Leadership Conference
320 Auburn Avenue, NE
Atlanta, GA 30303
(404) 522-1420
Email: contact@nationalsclc.org

Website: nationalsclc.org

Facebook: @nationalsclc

Twitter: @NationalSCLC

The Southern Christian Leadership Conference
is a civil rights organization born of the bus boycott
that is still active today.

Teaching Tolerance

400 Washington Avenue

Montgomery, AL 36104

(888) 414-7752

Website: splcenter.org/teaching-tolerance

Facebook: @SPLCenter

Twitter: @splcenter

A project of the Southern Poverty Law Center, Teaching Tolerance is a group dedicated to combatting prejudice among youth and promoting equality, inclusiveness, and equitable learning environments in the classroom.

Young People For (YP4)

1101 15th Street NW., Suite 600

Washington, D.C. 20005

Email: Youngpeoplefor@pfaw.org

Website: Youngpeoplefor.org

Facebook: youngpeoplefor

Twitter: @YP4

A project of People for the American Way that empowers young people to advocate for social justice in their communities.

Websites

Because of the changing nature of internet links, Rosen Publishing has developed an online list of websites related to the subject of this book. This site is updated regularly. Please use this link to access this list:

http://www.rosenlinks.com/COP/Hate

For Further Reading

Baldwin, James. *The Fire Next Time*. New York, NY: Vintage, 1992.

Bartoletti, Susan Campbell. *Hitler Youth: Growing Up in Hitler's Shadow*. New York, NY: Scholastic, 2005.

Bartoletti, Susan Campbell. *They Called Themselves the K.K.K.: The Birth of an American Terrorist Group*. New York, NY: HMH Books for Young Readers, 2014.

Branch, Taylor. *The King Years: Historic Moments in the Civil Rights Movement*. New York, NY: Simon & Schuster, 2013.

Coates, Ta-Nehisi. *Between the World and Me*. New York, NY: Spiegel and Grau, 2015.

Dunkell, Barbara, and Janell Broyles. *Frequently Asked Questions About Hate Crimes* (FAQ: Teen Life). New York, NY: Rosen Publishing, 2012.

Grinapol, Corrine. *Racial Profiling and Discrimination: Your Legal Rights* (Know Your Rights). New York, NY: Rosen Publishing, 2016.

Klein, Rebecca T. *Transgender Rights and Protections* (Transgender Life). New York, NY: Rosen Publishing, 2017.

Petrikowski, Nicki Peter. *Working for Tolerance and Social Change Through Service Learning* (Service Learning for Teens). New York, NY: Rosen Publishing, 2015.

Webber, Diane. *Totally Tolerant: Spotting and Stopping Prejudice*. New York, NY: Scholastic, 2008.

Yousafzai, Malala, and Christina Lamb. *I Am Malala: The Girl Who Stood Up for Education and Was Shot by the Taliban*. London, UK: Weidenfeld and Nicolson, 2013.

Zusak, Markus. *The Book Thief*. New York, NY: Alfred A. Knopf, 2007.

Bibliography

BBC News. "Portrait of a Girl Blogger." BBC News magazine, October 10, 2012. http://www.bbc.com/news/magazine-19899540.

Branch, Taylor. *The King Years: Historic Moments in the Civil Rights Movement.* New York, NY: Simon & Schuster, 2013.

CBC News. "Bullied Student Tickled Pink by Schoolmates T-Shirt Campaign." CBC News, September 18, 2007. http://www.cbc.ca/news/canada/bullied-student-tickled-pink-by-schoolmates-t-shirt-campaign-1.682221.

Chenoweth, Erica, and Maria J. Stephan. *Why Civil Resistance Works: The Strategic Logic of Nonviolent Conflict.* New York, NY: Columbia University Press, 2011.

Dozier, Rush W., Jr., *Why We Hate: Understanding, Curbing, and Eliminating Hate in Ourselves and Our World.* Chicago, IL: Contemporary Books, 2002.

Duggan, Maeve. "Online Harassment." Pew Research Center, October 22, 2014. http://www.pewinternet.org/2014/10/22/online-harassment.

Foxman, Abraham H., and Christopher Wolf. *Viral Hate: Containing Its Spread on the Internet.* New York, NY: St. Martin's Press, 2013.

Hardiman, David. "Toward a History of Nonviolence." Economic and Political Weekly,

June 8, 2013. http://www2.warwick.ac.uk/fac /arts/history/people/staff_index/dhardiman /nvr__history_-_epw_june_2013.pdf.

Hayes, Steven C. "The Orlando Massacre: Why We Hate: Science Shows Why and How We Can Use Love to Fight Hate." *Psychology Today*, June 13, 2016. https://www.psychologytoday.com /blog/get-out-your-mind/201606/the-orlando -massacre-why-we-hate.

Heard-Garris, Nia, and Danielle Erkoboni. "To Honor Dr. King, Pediatricians Offer Four Tips to Teach Kindness to Kids." The Conversation, January 12, 2017. https://theconversation.com /to-honor-dr-king-pediatricians-offer-four -tips-to-teach-kindness-to-kids-70620.

King, Martin Luther, Jr. "The Power of Nonviolence." Speech, June 4, 1957, University of California, Berkeley. *What So Proudly We Hail: The American Soul in Story, Speech, and Song.* http://www.whatsoproudlywehail.org /wp-content/uploads/2013/01/King_The -Power-of-Nonviolence_Link1.pdf?x65350.

Kustanowitz, Esther D. "Hate Speech in Your Social Media Feed? Try These Tips." *Jewish Journal*, October 27, 2016. http://jewishjournal.com /cover_story/212379/.

Levin, Jack, and Gardena Rabrenovic. *Why We Hate.* Amherst, NY: Prometheus Books, 2004.

Levin, Michael E., et al. "Examining the Role of Psychological Inflexibility, Perspective Taking, and Empathic Concern in Generalized Prejudice." *Journal of Applied Social Psychology,* October 13, 2015. http://onlinelibrary.wiley .com/doi/10.1111/jasp.12355/abstract.

Lucas, Fred. "Fake News Is Old News for Elections—and Never All That Dangerous." American Thinker, January 8, 2017. http:// www.americanthinker.com/blog/2017/01/fake _news_is_old_news_for_elections__and _never_all_that_dangerous.html.

Malkus, Mitchel. "What Happened After an Anti-Semitic Bomb Threat at My School." *Washington Post*, March 10, 2017. https:// www.washingtonpost.com/opinions/what -happened-after-an-anti-semitic-bomb -threat-at-my-school/2017/03/10/3ed50602 -05aa-11e7-b1e9-a05d3c21f7cf_story .html?utm_term=.73e8335ddb7c&wpisrc=nl _headlines&wpmm=1.

Meyer, Robinson. "The Rise of Progressive Fake News: The Disempowered Left Now Faces Its Own Kinds of Hoaxes and Fables." *The Atlantic,* February 3, 2017. https://www.theatlantic.com /technology/archive/2017/02/viva-la -resistance-content/515532.

Pinker, Steven. *Better Angels of Our Nature: Why Violence Has Declined*. New York, NY: Penguin, 2011.

Robson, David. "How to Avoid Falling for Lies and Fake News." BBC, February 11, 2017. http:// www.bbc.com/future/story/20170210-how-to -avoid-falling-for-lies-and-fake-news.

Toomey, Fred. "Data, the Speed of Light, and You." *Tech Crunch*, November 8, 2015. https:// techcrunch.com/2015/11/08/data-the-speed -of-light-and-you.

Topping, Alexandra. "Malala Yousafzai Accepts Nobel Peace Prize with Attack on Arms Spending." *Guardian*, December 10, 2014. https://www.theguardian.com/world/2014 /dec/10/malala-yousafzia-nobel-peace-prize -attack.

Index

About the Author

Avery Elizabeth Hurt is a journalist and author of many books for children and young adults. She is convinced that, despite occasional setbacks, the world is getting better—much better—and that we can have a world free of hate and intolerance if we are willing to keep working for it.

Photo Credits

Cover Mark Reinstein/Corbis News/Getty Images; p. 6 Daniel Leal-Olivas/AFP/Getty Images; p. 9 Mark Wilson/Getty Images; pp. 10–11 Image Source/Digital Vision/Thinkstock; pp. 14–15 Gareth Cattermole/Getty Images; p. 16 Mark Boster/Los Angeles Times/Getty Images; p. 20 Roland Neveu/LightRocket/Getty Images; p. 25 moodboard/Thinkstock; pp. 29, 67, 74–75 Hulton Archive/Getty Images; p. 30 Frank Dandridge/The LIFE Images Collection/Getty Images; p. 33 Ron Galella, Ltd./Ron Galella Collection/Getty Images; pp. 36–37 Jim Spellman/WireImage/Getty Images; pp. 40–41, 78–79 Bettmann/Getty Images; pp. 42–43 DGLimages/iStock/Thinkstock; pp. 46–47 Visions of America/Universal Images Group/Getty Images; p. 52 Gajus/iStock/Thinkstock; pp. 54–55, 64 Bloomberg/Getty Images; p. 57 innovatedcaptures/iStock/Thinkstock; p. 60 Sion Touhig/Getty Images; pp. 62–63 Andersen Ross/Blend Images/Thinkstock; pp. 68–69 NurPhoto/Getty Images; p. 81 Magdevski/iStock/Thinkstock; p. 85 geargodz/iStock/Thinkstock; pp. 88–89 BrianAJackson/iStock/Thinkstock; p. 90 Walter Sanders/The LIFE Picture Collection/Getty Images; pp. 92–93 borgogniels/iStock/Thinkstock; cover and interior pages background© iStockphoto.com/Sergei Dubrovski.

Design and Layout: Nicole Russo-Duca; Editor and Photo Research: Heather Moore Niver